Microsoft Visio 2016
Keyboard Shortcuts

For Windows

By

U. C-Abel Books.

All Rights Reserved

Table of Contents

Acknowledgement.

U. C-Abel Books will not take all the credits for Microsoft Visio 2016 keyboard shortcuts listed in this book, but shares it with Microsoft Corporation because some of the shortcut keys came from them and are "used with permission from Microsoft".

Dedication

This book is dedicated to computer users and lovers of keyboard shortcuts all over the world.

Introduction.

We enjoy using shortcut keys because they set us on a high plane that astonishes people around us when we work with them. As wonderful shortcuts users, the worst eyesore we witness in computing is to see somebody sluggishly struggling to execute a task through mouse usage when in actual sense shortcuts will help to save that person the time wasted. Most people have asked us to help them with a list of shortcut keys that can make them work as smartly as we do and that drove us into research to broaden our knowledge and truly help them as they demanded, that is the reason for the existence of this book. It is a great tool for lovers of shortcuts, and those who want to join the group.

Most times, the things we love don't come by easily. It is our love for keyboard shortcuts that made us to bear long sleepless nights like owls, just to make sure we get the best out of it, and it is the best we got that we are sharing with you in this book. You cannot be the same at computing after reading this book. The time you entrusted to our care is an expensive possession and we promise not to mess it up.

Thank you.

What to Know Before You Begin.

General Notes.

1. It is important to note that when using shortcuts to perform any command, you should make sure the target area is active, if not, you may get a wrong result. Example, if you want to highlight all texts, you must make sure the text field is active and if an object, make sure the object area is active. The active area is always known by the location where the cursor of your computer blinks.

2. Most of the keyboard shortcuts you will see in this book refer to the U.S. keyboard layout. Keys for other layouts might not correspond exactly to the keys on a U.S. keyboard.

3. The plus (+) signs that come in the middle of keyboard shortcuts simply mean the keys are meant to be combined or held down together not to be added as one of the shortcut keys. In a case where plus sign is needed; it will be duplicated (++).

4. For keyboard shortcuts in which you press one key immediately followed by another key, the keys are separated by a comma (,).

5. It is also important to note that the shortcut keys listed in this book are for Microsoft Visio 2016.

Short Forms Used in This Book and Their Full Meaning.

The following are short forms of keyboard shortcuts used in this Microsoft Visio 2016 Shortcuts book and their full meaning.

1.	Alt	-	Alternate Key
2.	Caps Lock	-	Caps Lock Key
3.	Ctrl	-	Control Key
4.	Esc	-	Escape Key
5.	F	-	Function Key
6.	Num Lock	-	Number Lock Key
7.	Shft	-	Shift Key
8.	Tab	-	Tabulate Key
9.	Win	-	Windows logo key
10.	Prt sc	-	Print Screen

CHAPTER 1.

Gathering The Basic Knowledge Of Keyboard Shortcuts.

Without the existence of the keyboard, there wouldn't have been anything like keyboard shortcuts, so in this chapter we will learn a little about keyboard before moving to keyboard shortcuts.

1. Definition of Computer Keyboard.
This is an input device that is used to send data to the computer memory.

Sketch of a Keyboard

1.1 Types of Keyboard.

i. Standard (Basic) Keyboard.
ii. Enhanced (Extended) Keyboard.

i. **Standard Keyboard:** This is a keyboard designed during the 1800s for mechanical typewriters with just 10 function keys (F keys) placed at the left side of it.
ii. **Enhanced Keyboard:** This is the current 101 to 102-key keyboard that is included in almost all the personal computers (PCs) of nowadays, which has 12 function keys at the top side of it.

Function Keys

Numeric Keys

Alphabetic keys

1.2 Segments of the keyboard

- Numeric keys
- Alphabetic keys
- Punctuation keys
- Windows Logo key.
- Function keys
- Special keys

Numeric Keys: Numeric keys are keys with numbers from **0 - 9**.

Alphabetic Keys: These are keys that have alphabets on them, ranging from **A-Z**.

Punctuation Keys: These are keys of the keyboard used for punctuation. Examples include comma, full stop, colon, question marks, hyphen etc.

Windows Logo Key: A key on Microsoft Computer keyboard with its logo displayed on it. Search for this ⊞ on your keyboard.

Function Keys: These are keys that have **F** on them which are usually combined with other keys. They are F1 - F12, and are also in the class called Special Keys.

Special Keys: These are keys that perform special functions. They include: Tab, Ctrl, Caps lock, Insert,

Prt sc, alt gr, Shift, Home, Num lock, Esc and many others. Special keys work according to the type of computer involved. In some keyboard layout, especially laptops, the keys that turn the speaker on/off, the one that increases/decreases volume, the key that turns the computer Wifi on/off are also special keys.

Other Special Keys Worthy of Note.

Enter Key: This is located at the right-hand corner of the keyboard. It is used to send messages to the computer to execute commands, in most cases it is used to mean "Ok" or "Go".

Escape Key (ESC): This is the first key on the upper left of the keyboard. It is used to cancel routines, close menus and select options such as **Save** according to circumstance.

Control Key (CTRL): It is located on the bottom row of the left and right hand side of the keyboard. They also work with the function keys to execute commands using Keyboard shortcuts (key combinations).

Alternate Key (ALT): It is located on the bottom row, very close to the CTRL key on both side of the keyboard. It enables many editing functions to be accomplished by using some keystroke combinations on the keyboard.

Shift Key: This adds to the functions of the function keys. In addition, it enables the use of alternative function of a particular button (key), especially, those with more than one function on a key. E.g. use of capital letters, symbols and numbers.

1.3. Selecting/Highlighting With the Keyboard.

This is a highlighting method or style where data is selected using the keyboard instead of a computer mouse.

To do this:

- Move your cursor to the text you want to highlight, make sure that area is active,
- Hold down the shift key with one finger
- Then use another finger to move the arrow key that points to the direction you want to highlight.

1.4 The Operating Modes Of The Keyboard.

Just like the mouse the keyboard has two operating modes. The two modes are Text Entering and Command Mode.

a. **Text Entering Mode:** this mode gives the operator/user the opportunity to type text.

b.   **Command Mode:** this is used to command the operating system/software/application to execute commands in certain ways.

2. Ways To Improve In Your Typing Skill.

1. Put Your Eyes Off The Keyboard.

This is the aspect of keyboard usage that many don't find funny because they always ask. "How can I put my eyes off the keyboard when I am running away from the occurrence of errors on my file?" My aim is to be fast, is this not going to slow me down?

Of course, there will be errors and at the same time your speed will slow down but the motive behind the introduction of this method is to make you faster than you are. Looking at your keyboard while you type can make you get a sore neck, it is better you learn to touch type because the more you type with your eyes fixed on the screen instead of the keyboard, the faster you become.

An alternative to keeping your eyes off your keyboard is to use the *"Das Keyboard Ultimate"*.

2. Errors Challenge You

It is better to fail than not to try at all. Not trying at all is an attribute of the weak and lazybones. When you make mistakes, try again because errors are opportunities for improvement.

3. Good Posture (Position Yourself Well).
Do not adopt an awkward position while typing. You should get everything on your desk organized or arranged before sitting to type. Your posture while typing contributes to your speed and productivity.

4. Practice
Here is the conclusion of everything said above. You have to practice your shortcuts constantly. The practice alone is a way of improvement. "Practice brings improvement". Practice always.

2.1 Software That Will Help You Improve In Your Typing Skill.

There are several Software programs for typing that both kids and adults can use for their typing skill. Here is a list of software that can help you improve in your typing: Mavis Beacon, Typing Instructor, Mucky Typing Adventure, Rapid Tying Tutor, Letter Chase Tying Tutor, Alice Touch Typing Tutor and many more. Personally, I recommend Mavis Beacon.

To learn typing with MAVIS BEACON, install Mavis Beacon software to your computer, start with keyboard lesson, then move to games. Games like **Penguin Crossing, Creature Lab** or **Space Junk** will help you become a professional in typing. Typing and keyboard shortcuts work hand-in-hand.

Sketch of a computer mouse

Right Mouse button

Scroll button

Left Mouse button

3. Mouse:

This is an oval-shaped portable input device with three buttons for scrolling, left clicking, and right clicking that enables work to be done effectively on a computer. The plural form of mouse is mice.

3.1 Types of Computer Mouse

- Mechanical Mouse
- Optical Mechanical Mouse (Optomechanical)
- Laser Mouse
- Optical Mouse

- BlueTrack Mouse

3.2 Forms of Clicking:

Left Clicking: This is the process of clicking the left side button of the mouse. It can be called *clicking* without the addition of *left*.

Right Clicking: It is the process of clicking the right side button of the mouse.

Double Clicking: It is the process of clicking the left side button two times (twice) and immediately.

Double clicking is used to select a word while thrice clicking is used to select a sentence or paragraph.

Scroll Button: It is the little key attached to the mouse that looks like a tiny wheel. It takes you up and down a page when moved.

3.3 Mouse Pad: This is a small soft mat that is placed under the mouse to make it have a free movement.

3.4 Laptop Mouse Touchpad

This unlike the mouse we explained above is not external, rather it is inbuilt (comes with a laptop computer). With the presence of a laptop mouse touchpad, an external mouse is not needed to use a laptop, except in a case where it is malfunctioning or the operator prefers to use external one for some reasons.

The laptop mouse touchpad is usually positioned at the end of the keyboard section of a laptop computer. It is rectangular in shape with two buttons positioned below it. The two buttons/keys are used for left and right clicking just like the external mouse. Some laptops come with four mouse keys. Two placed above the mouse for left and right clicking and two other keys placed below it for the same function.

4. Definition Of Keyboard Shortcuts.

Keyboard shortcuts are defined as a series of keys, sometimes with combination that execute tasks that typically involve the use of mouse or other input devices.

5. Why You Should Use Shortcuts.

1. One may not be able to use a computer mouse easily because of disability or pain.

2. One may not be able to see the mouse pointer as a result of vision impairment, in such case what will the person do? The answer is SHORTCUT.

3. Research has made it known that Extensive mouse usage is related to Repetitive Syndrome Injury (RSI) greatly than the use of keyboard.

4. Keyboard shortcuts speed up computer users, making learning them a worthwhile effort.

5. When performing a job that requires precision, it is wise that you use the keyboard instead of mouse, for instance, if you are dealing with Text Editing, it is better you handle it using keyboard shortcuts than spending more time with mouse alone.

6. Studies calculate that using keyboard shortcuts allows working 10 times faster than working with the mouse. The time you spend looking for the mouse and then getting the cursor to the position you want is lost! Reducing your work duration by 10 times brings you greater results.

5.1 Ways To Become A Lover Of Shortcuts.

1. Always have the urge to learn new shortcut keys associated with the programs you use.
2. Be happy whenever you learn a new shortcut.
3. Try as much as you can to apply the new shortcuts you learnt.
4. Always bear it in mind that learning new shortcuts is worth it.

5. Always remember that the use of keyboard shortcuts keeps people healthy while performing computing activities.

5.2 How To Learn New Shortcut Keys

1. Do a research for them: quick reference (a cheat sheet comprehensively compiled) can go a long way to help you improve.
2. Buy applications that show you keyboard shortcuts every time you execute an action with the mouse.
3. Disconnect your mouse if you must learn this fast.
4. Read user manuals and help topics (Whether offline or online).

5.3 Your Reward For Knowing Shortcut Keys.

1. You will get faster unimaginably.
2. Your level of efficiency will increase.
3. You will find it easy to use.
4. Opportunities are high that you will become an expert in what you do.
5. You won't have to go for **Office button**, click **New,** click **Blank and Recent** and click **Create** just to insert a fresh/blank page. **Ctrl +N** takes care of that in a second.

A Funny Note: Keyboard Shortcuts and Mousing are in a marital union with Keyboard Shortcuts being the head and it will be unfair for anybody to put asunder between them.

5.4 Why We Emphasize On The Use of Shortcuts.

You may never ditch your mouse completely unless you are ready to make your brain a box of keyboard shortcuts which will really be frustrating. Just imagine yourself learning all the shortcuts for the programs you use and its various versions. You shouldn't learn keyboard shortcuts that way.

Why we are emphasizing on the use of shortcuts is because mouse usage is becoming unusually common and unhealthy, too. So we just want to make sure both are combined so you can get fast, productive and healthy in your computing activities. All you need to know is just the most important ones associated with the programs you use.

CHAPTER 2.

15 (Fifteen) Special Keyboard Shortcuts.

The fifteen special keyboard shortcuts are fifteen (15) shortcut keys every computer user should know.

The following table contains the list of keyboard shortcuts every computer user should know.

1. **Ctrl + A:** Control plus A, highlights or selects everything you have in the environment where you are working.

   > *If you are like* **"Wow, the content of this document is large and there is no time to select all of it, besides, it's going to mount pressure on my computer?"** *Using the mouse for this is an outdated method of handling a task like selecting all, Ctrl+A will take care of that within seconds.*

2. **Ctrl + C:** Control plus C copies any highlighted or selected element within the work environment.

   > *Saves the time and stress which would have been used to right click and click again just to copy. Use ctrl+c.*

3. **Ctrl + N:** Control plus N opens a new window. *Instead of clicking* **File, New, blank/ template** *and another* **click**, *just press* ***Ctrl + N*** *and a fresh window will appear instantly.*

4. **Ctrl + O:** Control plus O opens a new program. *Use ctrl +O when you want to locate or open a file or program.*

5. **Ctrl + P:** Control plus P prints the active document. *Always use this to locate the printer dialog box and print.*

6. **Ctrl + S:** Control plus S saves a new document or file and changes made by the user. *Going for the mouse? Please stop! Don't use the mouse. Just press Ctrl+S and everything will be saved.*

7. **Ctrl +V:** Control plus V pastes copied elements into the active area of the program in use. *Using ctrl+V in a case like this Saves the time and stress of right clicking and clicking again just to paste.*

8. **Ctrl + W:** Control plus W is used to close the page you are working on when you want to leave the work environment.

> ***"There is a way Peace does this without using the mouse. Oh my God, why didn't I learn it then?"*** Don't worry, I have the answer, Peace presses Ctrl+W to close active windows.

9. **Ctrl + X:** Control plus X cuts elements (making the elements to disappear from their original place). The difference between cutting and deleting elements is that in Cutting, what was cut doesn't get lost permanently but prepares itself so that it can be pasted in another location selected by the user.

> *Use ctrl+x when you think* ***"this shouldn't be here and I can't stand the stress of retyping or redesigning it in the rightful place it belongs".***

10. **Ctrl + Y:** Control plus Y redoes an undone action.

> *Ctrl+Z brought back what you didn't need? Press Ctrl+ Y to remove it again.*

11. **Ctrl + Z:** Control plus Z undoes actions.

Can't find what you typed now or a picture you inserted, it suddenly disappeared or you mistakenly removed it? Press Ctrl+Z to bring it back.

12. **Alt + F4:** Alternative plus F4 closes active windows or items.

   *You don't need to move the mouse in order to close an active window, just press **Alt + F4** if you are done or don't want somebody who is coming to see what you are doing.*

13. **Ctrl + F6:** Control plus F6 Navigates between open windows, making it possible for a user to see what is happening in windows that are active.

   Are you working in Microsoft Word and want to find out if the other active window where your browser is loading a page is still progressing? Use Ctrl + F6.

14. **F1:** This displays the help window.

   *Is your computer malfunctioning? Use **F1** to find help when you don't know what next to do.*

15. **F12:** This enables user to make changes to an already saved document.

   F12 is the shortcut to use when you want to change the format in which you saved your existing document, password it, change its name, change the file location or destination, or make other changes to it. It will save your time.

CHAPTER 3.

 Keyboard Shortcuts In Visio 2016.

Definition of Program: Microsoft Visio is a diagramming and vector graphics application that was acquired by Microsoft in 2000. With Microsoft Visio, diagrams can be created with just a few clicks.

The following list contains keyboard shortcuts that will boost your productivity in Microsoft Visio.

Visio-Specific Tasks

Format text

TASK	SHORTCUT
Open the **Home** tab in the ribbon	ALT+H
Open the **Text** dialog box.	F11
Open the **Format Shape** task pane.	F3

Use the Snap & Glue features

TASK	SHORTCUT
Open the **Snap & Glue** dialog box.	ALT+F9

Group, rotate, and flip shapes

TASK	SHORTCUT
Group the selected shapes.	CTRL+G or CTRL+SHIFT+G
Ungroup shapes in the selected group.	CTRL+SHIFT+U
Bring the selected shape to the front.	CTRL+SHIFT+F
Send the selected shape to the back.	CTRL+SHIFT+B
Rotate the selected shape to the left.	CTRL+L
Rotate the selected shape to the right.	CTRL+R
Flip the selected shape horizontally.	CTRL+H
Flip the selected shape vertically.	CTRL+J
Open the **Align Shapes** dialog box for the selected shape.	F8

View drawing windows

TASK	SHORTCUT
Display the open drawing windows tiled vertically.	SHIFT+F7
Display the open drawing	CTRL+SHIFT+F7

windows tiled horizontally.	
Display the open drawing windows so that you can see the title of every window.	ALT+F7 or CTRL+ALT+F7

Visio-Specific Toolbars

Select tools

TASK	SHORTCUT
Switch the **Format Painter** tool on or off ( ).	CTRL+SHIFT+P
Select the **Pointer Tool** ( ).	CTRL+1
Select the **Connector** tool ( ).	CTRL+3
Select the connection point tool	CTRL+SHIFT+1
Select the text tool (**A**).	CTRL+2
Select the text box tool ( ).	CTRL+SHIFT+4

Select the drawing tools

TASK	SHORTCUT
Select the **Rectangle Tool** (□).	CTRL+8
Select the **Ellipse Tool** (○).	CTRL+9
Select the **Line Tool** ( ).	CTRL+6
Select the **Arc Tool** ( ).	CTRL+7
Select the **Freeform Tool** ( ).	CTRL+5
Select the **Pencil Tool** ( ).	CTRL+4

Crop a picture

TASK	SHORTCUT
Select the **Crop** tool ( ).	CTRL+SHIFT+2

21

Visio Shapes And Stencils

Move from shape to shape in a drawing page

TASK	SHORTCUT
Move from shape to shape on the drawing page. A dotted rectangle indicates the shape that has the focus. **Note:** You cannot move to shapes that are protected against selection or on a locked layer.	TAB
Move from shape to shape on the drawing page in reverse order.	SHIFT+TAB
Select a shape that has focus. **Note:** To select multiple shapes, press the TAB key to bring focus to the first shape you want to select, and then press ENTER. Hold down SHIFT while you press the TAB key to bring focus to another shape. When the focus rectangle is over the shape you want, press ENTER to add that shape to the selection. Repeat for each shape you want to select.	ENTER
Clear selection of or focus on a shape.	ESC
Switch between text edit mode and shape selection mode on a selected shape.	F2

Nudge a selected shape.	Arrow keys
Nudge a selected shape 1 pixel at a time. **Note:** SCROLL LOCK must be turned off.	SHIFT+Arrow keys

Work with master shapes in a stencil

TASK	SHORTCUT
Move between master shapes in a stencil.	Arrow keys
Move to the first master shape in a row of a stencil.	HOME
Move to the last master shape in a row of a stencil.	END
Move to the first master shape in a column of a stencil.	PAGE UP
Move to the last master shape in a column of a stencil.	PAGE DOWN
Copy the selected master shapes to the Clipboard.	CTRL+C
Paste the contents of the Clipboard to a new stencil. **Note:** The new stencil must first be opened for editing.	CTRL+V
Select all the master shapes in a stencil. **Note:** To select multiple master shapes (instead of all), press the arrow keys to bring focus to the	CTRL+A

first master shape you want. Hold down SHIFT while you press the arrow keys to bring focus to another master shape. When the focus rectangle is over the shape that you want, press ENTER to add that shape to the selection. Repeat for each shape that you want to select.	
Select or cancel selection of a master shape that has focus.	SHIFT+ENTER
Cancel the selection of master shapes in a stencil.	ESC
Insert the selected master shapes into the drawing.	CTRL+ENTER

Work with stencils in edit mode

TASK	SHORTCUT
Delete the selected master shape.	DELETE
Cut the selected master shape from the custom stencil and put it on the Clipboard.	CTRL+X
Rename the selected master shape.	F2

Online Help

Keyboard shortcuts for using the Help window

The Help window provides access to all Office Help content. The Help window displays topics and other Help content.

In the Help window

TASK	SHORTCUT
Open the Help window.	F1
Close the Help window.	ALT+F4
Switch between the Help window and the active program.	ALT+TAB
Go back to Visio Help Home.	ALT+HOME
Select the next item in the Help window.	TAB
Select the previous item in the Help window.	SHIFT+TAB
Perform the action for the selected item.	ENTER
Select the next hidden text or hyperlink, including **Show All** or **Hide All** at the top of a topic.	TAB
Select the previous hidden text or hyperlink.	SHIFT+TAB
Perform the action for the selected **Show All**, **Hide All**, hidden text, or hyperlink.	ENTER
Move back to the previous Help topic (**Back** button).	ALT+LEFT ARROW
Move forward to the next Help topic (**Forward** button).	ALT+RIGHT ARROW
Scroll small amounts up or down, respectively, within the currently displayed Help topic.	UP ARROW or DOWN ARROW
Scroll larger amounts up or down, respectively, within the currently displayed Help topic.	PAGE UP or PAGE DOWN

Microsoft Office Basics

Display and use windows

TASK	SHORTCUT
Switch to the next window.	ALT+TAB
Close the active window.	ALT+F4
Move to a task pane from another pane in the program window (clockwise direction). You may need to press F6 more than once. **Note:** If pressing F6 does not display the task pane you want, try pressing ALT to put focus on the ribbon.	F6
Maximize a selected window.	CTRL+F10
Restore the size of the Visio program window after you maximized it.	CTRL+F5
Copy a picture of the screen to the Clipboard.	PRINT SCREEN
Copy a picture of the selected window to the Clipboard.	ALT+PRINT SCREEN
For any window with an icon in its title bar (for example, a shapes window), display the window shortcut menu.	ALT+SPACEBAR

Open the **Page** dialog box.	SHIFT+F4
Open the **Reorder Pages** dialog box.	CTRL+ALT+P
Cycle the focus through open drawings.	CTRL+TAB or CTRL+F6
Cycle the focus through open drawings in reverse order.	CTRL+SHIFT+TAB or CTRL+SHIFT+F6
Cycle the focus through pages in a drawing, including any visible markup overlays.	CTRL+PAGE DOWN
Cycle the focus through pages in a drawing in reverse order.	CTRL+PAGE UP
When a task pane is active, select the next or previous option in the task pane.	TAB or SHIFT+TAB

Change or resize the font

TASK	SHORTCUT
Increase the font size of the selected text.	CTRL+SHIFT+>
Decrease the font size of the selected text.	CTRL+SHIFT+<

Move around in text or cells

TASK	SHORTCUT
Move one character to the left.	LEFT ARROW
Move one character to the	RIGHT ARROW

right.	
Move one line up.	UP ARROW
Move one line down.	DOWN ARROW
Move one word to the left.	CTRL+LEFT ARROW
Move one word to the right.	CTRL+RIGHT ARROW
Move to the end of a line.	END
Move to the beginning of a line.	HOME
Move up one paragraph.	CTRL+UP ARROW
Move down one paragraph.	CTRL+DOWN ARROW
Move to the end of a text box.	CTRL+END
Move to the beginning of a text box.	CTRL+HOME

Access and use task panes

TASK	SHORTCUT
Move to a task pane from another pane in the program window. (You may need to press F6 more than once.) **Note:** If pressing F6 does not display the task pane you want, try pressing ALT to put the focus on the ribbon and then pressing F6 to move to the task pane.	F6
When a task pane is active, select the next or previous option in the	TAB or SHIFT+TAB

task pane.	
Move among choices on a selected submenu; move among certain options in a group of options in a dialog box.	DOWN ARROW or UP ARROW
Open the selected menu, or perform the action assigned to the selected button.	SPACEBAR or ENTER
Open a shortcut menu	SHIFT+F10
When a menu or submenu is visible, select the first or last command, respectively, on the menu or submenu.	HOME or END

Float or anchor task panes

1. Press F6 repeatedly to select the task pane that you want.
2. Press ALT+SPACEBAR to open the menu for that task pane.
3. Press the DOWN ARROW key to select the **Float Window** command, and then press ENTER.

Use dialog boxes

TASK	SHORTCUT
Move to the next option or option group.	TAB
Move to the previous option or option group.	SHIFT+TAB
Switch to the next tab in a dialog box.	CTRL+TAB

Switch to the previous tab in a dialog box.	CTRL+SHIFT+TAB
Move between options in an open drop-down list, or between options in a group of options.	Arrow keys
Perform the action assigned to the selected button; select or clear the selected check box.	SPACEBAR
Open the list if it is closed and move to that option in the list.	First letter of an option in a drop-down list
Select an option; select or clear a check box.	ALT+ the letter underlined in an option
Open a selected drop-down list.	ALT+DOWN ARROW
Close a selected drop-down list; cancel a command and close a dialog box.	ESC
Perform the action assigned to a default button in a dialog box.	ENTER

Use edit boxes within dialog boxes

An edit box is a blank in which you type or paste an entry, such as your user name or the path of a folder.

TASK	SHORTCUT
Move to the beginning of the entry.	HOME

Move to the end of the entry.	END
Move one character to the left or right.	LEFT ARROW or RIGHT ARROW
Move one word to the left.	CTRL+LEFT ARROW
Move one word to the right.	CTRL+RIGHT ARROW
Select or cancel selection one character to the left.	SHIFT+LEFT ARROW
Select or cancel selection one character to the right.	SHIFT+RIGHT ARROW
Select or cancel selection one word to the left.	CTRL+SHIFT+LEFT ARROW
Select or cancel selection one word to the right.	CTRL+SHIFT+RIGHT ARROW
Select from the insertion point to the beginning of the entry.	SHIFT+HOME
Select from the insertion point to the end of the entry.	SHIFT+END

Use the Open and Save As dialog boxes

TASK	SHORTCUT
Move to the next option or option group.	TAB
Move to the previous option or	SHIFT+TAB

option group.	
Move between options in an open drop-down list, or between options in a group of options.	Arrow keys
Perform the action assigned to the selected button	ENTER, SPACEBAR
Move to the **Save as type** list in the **Save As** dialog box	ALT+T
Move to the **File name** box	ALT+N
Move to the file type list in the **Open** dialog box	ALT+T
Open a selected file in the **Open** dialog box	ALT+O
Save the current file in the **Save** dialog box	ALT+S
Open a selected drop-down list.	ALT+DOWN ARROW
Close a selected drop-down list; cancel a command and close a dialog box.	ESC
Update the file list	F5
Display a shortcut menu for a selected item such as a folder or file	SHIFT+F10

Text

Edit text

TASK	SHORTCUT
Move to the next or previous character, respectively, in a line of	RIGHT ARROW or LEFT ARROW

text.	
Move to the next or previous line of text, respectively.	DOWN ARROW or UP ARROW
Move to the next or previous word, respectively, in a line of text.	CTRL+RIGHT ARROW or CTRL+LEFT ARROW
Move to the next or previous paragraph, respectively.	CTRL+DOWN ARROW or CTRL+UP ARROW
Select all the text in a text block.	CTRL+A
Select the next or previous character, respectively.	SHIFT+RIGHT ARROW or SHIFT+LEFT ARROW
Select the next or previous word, respectively.	CTRL+SHIFT+RIGHT ARROW or CTRL+SHIFT+LEFT ARROW
Select the next or previous line, respectively.	SHIFT+DOWN ARROW or SHIFT+UP ARROW
Select the next or previous paragraph, respectively.	CTRL+SHIFT+DOWN ARROW or CTRL+SHIFT+UP ARROW
Delete the previous word.	CTRL+BACKSPACE
Replace the selected text with the field height. If no text is selected, replace all	CTRL+SHIFT+H

text with the field height for the selected shape.	

Format text

TASK	SHORTCUT
Turn bold (**B**) on or off.	CTRL+B
Turn italic (*I*) on or off.	CTRL+I
Turn underline (U) on or off.	CTRL+U
Turn double underline on or off.	CTRL+SHIFT+D
Turn all caps on or off.	CTRL+SHIFT+A
Turn small caps on or off.	CTRL+SHIFT+K
Turn subscript (x_2) on or off.	CTRL+=
Turn superscript (x^2) on or off.	CTRL+SHIFT+=
Increase the font size of the selected text.	CTRL+SHIFT+>
Decrease the font size of the selected text.	CTRL+SHIFT+<

Align text

TASK	SHORTCUT
Align text left.	CTRL+SHIFT+L
Center text horizontally.	CTRL+SHIFT+C
Align text right.	CTRL+SHIFT+R
Justify text horizontally.	CTRL+SHIFT+J
Top-align text vertically.	CTRL+SHIFT+T
Center text vertically.	CTRL+SHIFT+M
Bottom-align text vertically.	CTRL+SHIFT+V

Zoom and Navigation

Navigate the Ribbon

1. Press ALT.

   The KeyTips are displayed over each feature that is available in the current view.

2. Press the letter shown in the KeyTip over the feature that you want to use.
3. Depending on which letter you press, you may be shown additional KeyTips. For example, if the **Home** tab is active and you press N, the **Insert** tab is displayed, along with the KeyTips for the groups on that tab.
4. Continue pressing letters until you press the letter of the command or control that you want to use. In some cases, you must first press the letter of the group that contains the command. For example, if the **Home** tab is active, press ALT+H, F, S will take you to the **Size** list box in the **Font** group.

   Note: To cancel the action that you are taking and hide the KeyTips, press ALT.

Zoom

TASK	SHORTCUT
Zoom in.	ALT+F6
Zoom out.	ALT+SHIFT+F6
Fit to window	CTRL+SHIFT+W

Move around in full-screen view

Use these keyboard shortcuts to move between Visio and another program or page when you are in full-screen view.

TASK	SHORTCUT
Enter full-screen view	F5
Exit full-screen view	ESC
Open the next page in the drawing.	PAGE DOWN
Return to the previous page in the drawing.	PAGE UP

Move around a Web page drawing

TASK	SHORTCUT
Cycle the focus through the left frame, the drawing, and shapes on the drawing that contain shape data, hyperlinks, and the address bar.	TAB
Activate the hyperlink for the shape or hyperlink on the drawing that has focus.	ENTER

Customer's Page.

This page is for customers who enjoyed Microsoft Visio 2016 Keyboard Shortcuts For Windows.

Dearly beloved customer, please leave a review behind if you enjoyed this book or found it helpful. It will be highly appreciated, thank you.

Other Books By This Publisher.

S/N	Title	Series
Series A: Limits Breaking Quotes.		
1	Discover Your Key Christian Quotes	Limits Breaking Quotes
Series B: Shortcut Matters.		
1	Windows 7 Shortcuts	Shortcut Matters
2	Windows 7 Shortcuts & Tips	Shortcut Matters
3	Windows 8.1 Shortcuts	Shortcut Matters
4	Windows 10 Shortcut Keys	Shortcut Matters
5	Microsoft Office 2007 Keyboard Shortcuts For Windows.	Shortcut Matters
6	Microsoft Office 2010 Shortcuts For Windows.	Shortcut Matters
7	Microsoft Office 2013 Shortcuts For Windows.	Shortcut Matters
Series C: Teach Yourself.		
1	Teach Yourself Computer Fundamentals	Teach Yourself
Series D: For Painless Publishing		
1	Self-Publish it with CreateSpace.	For Painless Publishing
2	Where is my money? Now solved for Kindle and CreateSpace	For Painless Publishing
3	Describe it on Amazon	For Painless Publishing
4	How To Market That Book.	For Painless Publishing

www.ingramcontent.com/pod-product-compliance
Lightning Source LLC
Chambersburg PA
CBHW070415190526
45169CB00003B/1273